Homeland Nostalgia: The Cook's Soup Pot

By

Tochi Brown

i

Text: Cambria

Design: One Thought, Inc.

Photos and artwork: One Thought, Inc. and Tochi Brown.

Cover illustration: Courtesy of CreateSpace

Author photo: © Tochi Brown Adimiche

The short stories (For Better, For Abayomi; The Village Christmas Dance, Continued; Sunday-Sunday Merecin; The Man at Bar Beach) have been previously published online on tochi.us and Facebook.com in slightly different editions.

Library of Congress Cataloging-in-Publication Data

Homeland Nostalgia: The Cook's Soup Pot

     by Tochi Brown

ISBN 978-097-60659-4-4 (Paperback)

1. Creative writing. 2. Narration-Rhetoric. 3. College readers. 4. English language-Rhetoric

An Imprint of One Thought Press

P O Box 130938, The Woodlands, TX 77393, USA

http:// onethought.us

This book is for all my | sorors | fraters |

- Thank you for being there for me all the way and through the ages.

- Thank you for bringing me back to the kitchen.

I love you dearly.

Table of Contents

Introduction

Why do I write?

To share information, experiences and ideas, of course. Most importantly though, to incite my reader to think. Yes, *think*. Thinking has now become a conscious mental exercise for many; painful and only indulged in when absolutely necessary when there is no one else available to tell us what to think or do. Thinking has become, I believe, something that must be scheduled and fervidly practiced if one is to continue making intelligent decisions about the world around us.

Somewhere in the back of my nebulous thoughts I agreed with myself that I was going to write about my recent experiences in Nigeria. As I had been 'prepped' by my Nigerian friends in the US and Canada – Don't let people know that you're from the States! Don't trust anybody! Don't eat just anywhere! Don't drink the water! Don't be without lots of money! Don't stay with relatives! Don't travel at night! Don't sleep in the village! You will be abused/cheated/robbed/beaten/used for juju rituals! Don't stay for too long! – I proceeded, as was my nature to do, to break every injunction and advice and immerse myself in the diverse experiences that presented themselves to me. I have not died – yet. I have not gone insane – yet. I have not fled – yet!

No one really knows, save for the cook, what is in the soup. And it is the self-same cook who dishes out the contents of the pot. You get what you get. So it has been with my long visit to this country. I had no control over the environment. After a while, I stopped trying to rationalize and understand everything. I relaxed. I got what I got.

Hence this little book, Homeland Nostalgia: The Cook's Soup Pot... this collage of creative writing that has been fueled by fact, fiction and fantasy. Suspending what I knew and what I believed - I often didn't know where one ended and the other began. Ultimately, it didn't matter as much as sharing the experiences.

Thus, the book now in your hands. Therefore, so be it.

Tochi Brown

Lagos, Nigeria.

The Train Station

I stand on the platform, waiting, looking down the tracks expectantly, like I know for sure that my train will arrive anytime now. But it appears that the train left the station without me, or never arrived in the first place. I look at myself in the reflection of the station glasses: tall, strong, visible; acceptably pretty in the right clothes and with the right makeup. I wonder if I am at the right station; if I ought to travel; if I want to travel in the first place; if it is God's will for me to travel at all. I focus on the last thought: Maybe train travel is not destined for me. Where would I be headed anyhow? There are an infinite number of trains, destinations, and combinations of both.

I look at the faces others as they pass me by. Some just got off their trains, some are looking to change destinations; others seek to board theirs, just like me. I wonder what they all are thinking their chances of boarding are, how early in the morning they had to rise to make it to the station, what preparations they made, what secrets they hide.

I espy a place to sit, recently vacated. I make a beeline for it. Out of nowhere, a man appears and occupies the seat. He looks up to glare at me; how dare I arrogate the thought of sitting there? I sigh angrily and turn around to look at my reflection again in the windows.

I look at the tracks again, willing my train – any train – to pull up and take me away from here. The silence is piercing my soul. I look at my luggage: Did I pack too much? I look at myself in the glass again: Am I too much?

A rumble in the distance! A renewed bustle of activity on the platform as people surge forward, looking this way and that, up and down the tracks. I don't know whether to surge forward with them, or to hold back and wait my turn. The headlight of a train appears on the distance horizon. My heart skips a beat. I reach down and grab the handles of my luggage. The rumble of the train grows louder. I'm sure I want to travel, I tell myself. The train stops, still far away from the station. With everyone else, I watch expectantly, hopefully, reverentially for the train to continue its approach. But there is a loud "Clang! Clang! Clang! Clang!" The train tracks are switched. The train proceeds, slowly at first, and then gathers momentum. I watch as the train speeds by the platform, its engineer looking straight ahead like no one was even there.

A crowd murmurs loudly, disappointed. Deflated, I look around for a seat. I find one, recently vacated by a fellow expectant passenger. I make a beeline for it. Out of nowhere, a man appears and occupies the seat. He looks up to glare at me; how dare I arrogate the thought of sitting there? I sigh angrily and turn around to look at my reflection again in the station windows.

A couple of hours pass by. No train in sight or sound. I'm tired of standing. Off to the side, I arrange my luggage on the floor, making a seat for myself to sink down upon. People mill around me. I'm sweating profusely in the evening heat. Some step on my clothes and others kick me as they pass by. They don't care at all. I get tired of shouting at them to mind me. I get tired of paying attention to them.

I overhear snippets of conversations as people walk by. "I traveled on that train; it was no good!" "That trip was good while it lasted." "I've been waiting a long while to board a train." "I'm tired of waiting for a train." And so forth.

Another train sedately approaches the station. As it comes to a stop, I scramble to my feet. I don't care about my smudged and sweaty clothes anymore. I don't care where it's headed – I just want to board that train! I jostle and push with everyone else at one of the coach doors. I don't even know what class it is. A couple of women make it up the stairs and disappear into the coach. I get excited. I could be next. I should be next! Some more shoving and shouting, the doors of the trains begin to close. I get frantic. My luggage begins to slip from my sweaty hands. I don't care anymore. I push my way forward. The door shuts in my face. I am in shocked disbelief. What just happened here?

The train moves slowly but surely out of the station. Head pounding with pain, I fight back tears and swallow the lump in my throat. Demoralized, I look around for a vacant seat. I find one; I make a beeline for it. Out of nowhere, a man appears and occupies the seat. He looks up to glare at me; how dare I arrogate the

2

thought of sitting there? Angry tears trickle down my cheeks. I turn around to look at my reflection in the station windows.

1. Psst. [Whistle.]

2. Hey, come here.

3. [Kissing sound.]

4. Sister.

5. Aunty.

6. Madam.

7. Mummy. (I am here now, greatly aided by my grey.)

8. Mama.

It was about 9:30 p.m. and pretty dark outside. I needed directions to her house in Enugu. I stood some distance away from my party at the entrance to the Golden Palace Hotel.

"How do I get to your house from here?"

"Where are you?" she demanded.

"I'm in Independence Layout."

"Where?"

"Independence Layout!"

"Did you say Independence Layout?" she demanded again.

"Yes, I said I'm in Independence Layout!"

"Eh, from Independence Layout, take a *taguzi*. Tell them you are going to Emene."

"Okay, I should take a taxi."

"Eh, yes. Take a *taguzi*. Tell them you want a drop. Tell the *taguzi* driver that you are going to the police station in Emene. Everybody knows the police station in Emene. When you get to the police station call me and give the phone to the *taguzi* driver so that I can direct him further."

"Why can't you just give me all the details now, so that I can tell the taxi driver myself?"

"No, give the phone to the *taguzi* driver!" she yelled.

My voice rose an octave. "I don't want to give my phone to any taxi driver! Just tell me everything!"

The people over at the hotel entrance looked over my way. One of them, Basil, started walking towards me, a worried look on his face. I lowered my voice.

"Look, Oluchi, I have to go. When I get to the police station, I will get down from the taxi and call you to come and get me."

"No, you will get lost! Listen to me! This is not Independence Layout! Let me talk to the *taguzi* driver so that I can direct him on how to get to my house!"

Basil walked up to me. "Is everything alright?"

2

"Yes," I forced a bright smile at him. "I'm on the phone with my cousin Oluchi. She's giving me directions on how to get to her house."

"Where does she live?"

"In Emene," I replied.

"Who are you talking to?" Oluchi demanded over the phone.

"Oh, I don't even know where that is," Basil responded. "Do you know how to get there?"

"I'll take a taxi. That shouldn't be a problem," I assured him.

"Who are you talking to?" she demanded again. "Is that the *taguzi* driver?"

"No, it's not the taxi driver. It's a friend."

"Is he going to bring you to Emene? Ask him if he can bring you to Emene so that I can give him directions!" she yelled at me.

"No, he's not going to Emene. He doesn't live here."

"Well, give him the phone let me tell him how to help you get to Emene from Independence Layout!" she insisted.

Exasperated, I handed the phone over to Basil. Eyebrows lifted, he took the phone from me.

"Hello?" he said.

"Are you bringing my cousin to Emene?" she asked.

"No. I don't live here myself," he replied.

"Eh? You don't live in Enugu?"

"No I don't live in Enugu."

"Where are you from?" Oluchi asked.

Basil smiled. "I'm from Abuja."

"So you are an Hausa man?" she accused him.

He was startled. "No, I'm not an Hausa man."

"But you live in Hausa land!" she countered.

"There are various tribes living in Abuja," he responded.

Oluchi changed tack. "So you know my sister?" she queried.

"Yes, I know your sister. She is my friend."

3

"Okay, so you are my sister's friend. So she met you in Abuja, eh?"

Basil remained silent.

"Are you people in Independence Layout now?"

"Yes, we are in Independence Layout right now," he affirmed.

"Okay, can you help her find a *taguzi* to bring her to Emene?"

"Yes, I can help her find a taxi. Is that where you live?"

"Yes, I live in Emene. Tell the *taguzi* driver that it is a drop. Tell the driver to bring her to the police station in Emene. You know where the police station in Emene is, right?"

"No, I don't know the police station in Emene. I don't live here."

"Okay, tell the *taguzi* driver to take her to the police station in Emene. When he reaches there, call me so that I can direct you further to my house. Do you hear what I'm saying?" Oluchi yelled.

"Yes, I hear you. I will tell the taxi driver what you said." Basil rolled his eyes at me.

"Make sure the driver brings her straight to the police station in Emene. It is dark now. She doesn't know any where in Enugu. She doesn't live here. My house is not far from the police station. Give your phone to the *taguzi* driver when you get to the police station. I will tell him how to get to my house from there."

"Yes, ma, I will do just that. I will give it to him."

"Okay, thank you oh. Thank you very much. I will be expecting you. Don't forget. It's the police station in Emene."

"No, I won't forget. Thank you, ma. She is coming now. Bye-bye."

Basil hung up and turned to me. "Accept my sympathies."

America Emerged

I came to see for myself

If my Nigeria still existed.

Wandering through dark shopping malls,

              faux-genteel WiFi cafes

Now rife with Lucky Goldstar televisions,

      iPads,

      Samsung smartphones.

And those same jaded concrete houses,

      muddy marketplaces,

      chaotic bus parks,

And more than one fly-ridden *bukateria*

I left so many years ago –

                    America emerged, unheeding.

I fled to the countryside,

A believer that my Nigeria would still abide.

            For where?

The fruit seller shed set like a multicolored plastic pendant

Upon the common bosom of the same old dull garbage

Now fluttered her Hollywood lashes in invitation to buy.

                    America unsinking.

The bewigged grandmother straddled across a speeding *okada*

Flung sweat from her forehead with her finger

Wrapper hitched high upon her unrepentant thigh.

                    America unblinking.

Elsewhere, the young wife with child removed her patterned hijab

So that she could extend her hennaed fingers

For the acquisition of shiny, new acrylic nails.

                    America unthinking.

My Nigeria now wants to

     Be like me,

     Talk like me,

     Walk like me

     Even f*** with me.

            Chei!

I came to see for myself

If my Nigeria still existed

Instead, America emerged.

I walk, in a few hours, the many years of my youth here. Hard as I try, few places are familiar. Everything appears so commercialized. People hurry past me, unsmiling, disinterested, barely polite... unless my money is coming their way. So I try my darndest best not to send it.

A tricycle cab drops me off by the primary school that used to be smack dab in the middle of Aladinma Housing Estate. Contrary to the dismal reports I had received, pupils are plentiful, and there are blocks of classrooms in bright colors. There are small heaps of garbage in the gutters framing the playground, parts of which have been appropriated into private cassava farms. Nothing new here.

I walk along the street where I used to live with my guardian. I already know that the prison-house is gone; now it has been replaced with a bungalow of indeterminate usage. I keep on walking, take a turn, and then take another turn. I remember and see the children and their families who used to live around here.

Everywhere, it seems there are young people. The boys are lithe, impatient and Americanized. The girls are wearing the shoes I so desperately wished I had when I was their age.

They are how I remember myself to be: wanting, hungry, eager to please, bright-eyed, flippant, skinny, gaudily garbed, sharp, ubiquitous.	*How I perceive myself to be now: wanting, hungry, eager to please, bright-eyed, flippant, muscular, unfashionably garbed, forgetful, wandering.*

I keep on moving.

I reach a fork in the road. Somewhere to the left was Miss Julianna's house. She fed, dressed and counseled me. I used to wish that she were my mother. Does she still live there? Twenty-eight years later, my spirit still needs to be fed, dressed and counseled. I go looking for her.

Sumptuous dinner consumed, my cousins and I left Dede Noel's house and strolled along the path between family compounds to Dede Israel's house. His home was a faded faux-colonial style bungalow, a greyish-blue structure in the fast fading light. Mango and orange trees framed the sides of the small clearing in the front. To the left, a sooty black round iron pot, sat on a tripod of stones, vigorously boiling over firewood flames.

As usual, Dede Israel sat in his wooden low-slung chair in the front porch. He appeared to be daydreaming or something. A stone's throw distant, we greeted him in unison: "*Mazi* oooo!"

He looked our way with foggy eyes and bared almost toothless gums. "My children, how are you?"

"We are fine", we responded together again.

Dede Israel hummed and cleared his throat.

"Whose children are you?" he queried.

There was silence as we looked at one another, waiting for someone to speak first.

"We are Dede Noel's children," one of us finally volunteered.

"Children of Noel? Eh, my children, you are welcome."

We murmured assent as we sat down on the long wooden bench beside him. As we sat in silence, a couple of minutes later there was a rustle at the front door curtain. His wife, Ma Cyril, came out to the verandah and looked at us with a tired smile.

"Noel's children, *ndewo*! Welcome."

"Mama, good evening ma" we responded.

She went back indoors. We remained sitting in silence with Dede Israel. He appeared to continue his evening reveries, with lips moving soundlessly and eyes focused on some horizon.

Eventually, more people trickled in as the darkness lowered its mantle upon the village. Diverse greetings were offered, accepted and returned. As youngsters, we had to give up our seats for the adults. Looking around, I found a small wooden stool near the fire. I sat down quietly, mouse-like, so as not to draw attention to my find. I didn't want to give my seat up to yet another older relative. My cousins found places on the ground somewhere.

Aunt Dahlia, Brother Cyril's wife, silently appeared beside me. She stood near the fire. I looked up at her. The flames barely illuminated her round face and her modest native garb. Smiling cautiously, she greeted everyone present in her beautifully modulated tone: "*Mazi nine, ndewo!*"

There was a murmur of responses. Dede Israel turned his eyes toward her, but didn't utter a sound.

"Dede Israel, good evening sir!" she firmly called out to him.

He grunted and looked away.

She stood there, visible and persistent; he sat there, unwelcoming and intractable. The rest of us sat there between the two: uncomfortable, silent, and looking at neither.

I wondered if others were thinking the same thing that I was thinking. It was well known in the extended family that Aunt Dahlia, an Efik woman – a *Calabar* woman – was not his preference for his first son, Cyril. Rumor had it that once a man got involved with a *Calabar* woman, he was to be considered lost to his family. The potent combination of her cooking, the way she walked, talked and looked at a man – including her fabled sexual skills taught to her from a very tender age – were all calculated to mesmerize, weaken and entrap men forever. Consequently, all of the man's resources and attention, rightfully meant for his own relatives, would now be lavished on her and her family.

In Dede Israel's world, the Efik, the Ibibio, the Annang peoples – in short, the *Calabar people* – all of them were the cannibalistic Mmong people. According to him, the Mmong were all wicked, heartless and bloodthirsty. He would know: he used to trade with them back in the day when he was a young, strapping fellow living in Aba.

Eventually, he turned his almost sightless eyes toward her person again.

"*Nwanyi Mmong*, who are you going to eat tonight as we sleep?"

General laughter rose from those present. Someone mildly admonished Dede Israel. Another told Aunt Dahlia not to mind his jokes. I looked again at her face. Her ingratiating smile had vanished, replaced by a an expressionless, yet observant, mien.

Someone asked, "Dede Israel, what have the Mmong ever done to you?"

Dede Israel frowned, then responded: "I keep telling you people that the Mmong are terrible people. You know, I used to trade with them back when I lived in Aba. I wasn't married then, even though many women sought me out in those days for my prowess. It was very hard for them to leave me alone."

He continued, "Back then I used to live with Okoli Igwe; you know, Okoli Igwe of Umuezuma, the son of Akachi Okoli, who lived by the Oye market of Umuezuma."

He coughed violently, hacked, spat out the phlegm.

"Back then, we used to go to the Mmong market to buy palm kernels. Okoli drove the lorry we used to load the palm kernels. I did the transactions because I knew how to negotiate very well."

"If there is any gossip about me as a man, it is due to the Mmong people. One day I was a full-bodied, red-blooded man; the next, I had to search myself for the next three months. Thank God that Mama Cyril is an Aro woman, otherwise the story would have been told much differently."

It became obvious that the Mmong story was about to be told again. We now waited in silence to hear the latest version of it.

"On the day that the Mmong almost ate me, Okoli Igwe and I had driven down to buy the palm kernels as usual. However, as we were loading our lorry with the heads of palm kernels, I overheard the Mmong men standing nearby debate among themselves as to who, between Okoli and I, had more fat and would be tastier. I was shocked, but I kept my composure. They didn't know that I understood everything that they were saying!"

Someone in the night audience exclaimed, "Eh? They wanted to eat whom? *Tufiakwa*! God forbid evil! To eat the flesh of your fellow human being!"

The rest of us remained silent.

"Yes," continued Dede Israel, "they ate their fellow human beings like goat meat. But I did not let them know that I knew what they were planning. I kept listening. They planned to grab one of us as soon as more of them arrived. Very surreptitiously, I whispered in Igbo to Okoli what was afoot. I told his that what we should do was continue loading the heads of palm kernel; as soon as we got to the last four or so, he should go start up the lorry. I would quickly toss in the last heads and, as soon as I banged the side of the lorry, he should take off immediately without looking back. By then, I would have jumped onto the back of the lorry."

"Okoli Igwe agreed. The Mmong were watching us, speaking among themselves. They were discussing how big we were and tasty our meat would taste."

"We got down to four heads of palm kernels. I gave a signal to Okoli Igwe. He strolled to the front of the lorry, opened the driver's side door, got in and started the lorry. I grabbed a palm kernel head. As I rose to swing it onto the back of the lorry, the Mmong men started closing in on me in a hurry. I abandoned the last two heads and banged on the side of the lorry. Okoli engaged the gear and the lorry lurched forward, real fast. I grabbed the top of the back tailgate to swing myself up... but my hand slipped. I fell to the ground. The lorry raced away."

Mama Cyril swept aside the front door curtain and came out onto the verandah. She bustled to her husband's side and stood quietly.

Dede Israel continued. "The Mmong men, about ten of them, pounced on me. They pinned me to the ground, shouting with joy. I didn't know what to do. I thought it was the end of my life. However, a voice inside me told me to swallow my breath and play dead. So, closing my eyes, I swallowed my breath into my belly. I stopped breathing."

"In the meantime, the Mmong men carried me to their marketplace. Very soon, through the crack of my eyelids, I saw a crowd of both men and women gather around me. I was stripped naked as the day I was born! They were all excited and happy. Fresh meat had arrived!"

"However, an argument ensued among some of the men present. As I listened, I came to understand that they were arguing over my testicles as to who rightfully owned that portion of the meat. My own testicles! One of them was handling my testicles, squeezing them and turning them this way and that, over and over again. Can you imagine men handling and squeezing your testicles like they were mangoes displayed for sale? But I had swallowed my breath, so I could remain motionless."

"One of the Mmong men argued that I had to be butchered immediately, as it appeared to them that I had already died of fright. A couple of others kept insisting that my testicles were rightfully theirs, and that they would not participate if they were not assigned that portion beforehand. As they argued back and forth, I felt my manhood being lifted and massaged with something like a salve. Within minutes, I felt as if my organs were being roasted on an open flame. I almost came alive with pain. But I had to remain alive and figure out my escape. I had to continue playing dead."

"Next, as the Mmong continued arguing, I heard the sound of a lorry approaching us. A loud murmur, then confusion ensued. I heard people running away. Opening my eyes and retrieving my breath, I recognized Okoli Igwe and several *kotuma*! They had come to rescue me!"

"I jumped up, shouted, and ran towards them. My penis and testicles were on fire. By that time, the Mmong were nowhere to be seen. Their market became naked of people. Okoli Igwe returned to save me from the hands of the Mmong that day."

"Okoli Igwe and I returned to Aba later that night. It took me several months to recover from my ordeal at the hands of the Mmong people. Look at Cyril, my firstborn son. If not for Akachi Okoli, Okoli Igwe's father, and his herbal ministrations, my children would not look like they were my own offspring at all."

"I know that times have changed, and children now do what they want to do. I'm not saying that people shouldn't do what they want to do; after all, what is paramount is the obedience to custom. But what I want to say is that the Mmong should not be allowed to mingle freely with others. What is already in the blood will always remain in the blood. I know how I got my children. That's all I'm saying."

Wordlessly, I looked up as Mama Cyril and Aunt Dahlia exchanged glances. The former smirked; the latter walked away.

I looked over at the pot over the fire. The embers of the leftover coals glowed a dull orange in the pitch darkness. I wondered to myself: Was this story about his mangled manliness, or distrusting his daughter-in-law?

Example #1:

Early in the morning, Favor took out the tape measure from his pocket, looked both ways to confirm that no one was watching him in the food pantry, then he carefully measured the cut yam tuber lying on the floor.

He squinted at the reading: 23 cm. He mentally compared this figure to yester-night's figure of 57 cm. *Mcheew!* He kissed his teeth in part disgust, part anger. It was as he suspected: his younger cousins were eating yam every day. What did they take him for, a free food provider?

He decided that he was going to stop buying yams for the rest of the year.

Example #2:

Favor was curious to know what his cousin left behind in the guest room when she traveled that morning to Abuja. He tried the door. It was locked. Thinking quickly, he sent her a text message: "You left the air conditioner on in the guest room."

A couple of minutes later, the response came: "That is strange. However, the key is hidden in the arm of the sofa near the door."

Favor quickly retrieved the key and opened the door. Espying his cousin's luggage, he quickly went through them to ascertain that none of his stuff was hidden in them.

Next he went to the bathroom, where he saw the white towel he had loaned her. He quickly examined it and found it to be freshly laundered. He took it.

Example #3:

"Ping! Ping!" It was a new text message. Favor quickly checked his phone. His cousin needed to be picked up from the airport in four hours' time. He texted her back with a promise to pick her up promptly.

Four hours and fifteen minutes later, she called him. "Where are you? I'm at the airport!"

"Sorry, I can't make it after all", Favor replied. "Could you get a taxi instead?"

"The taxis here are terribly expensive! They are charging about five times the usual rate."

Favor thought about this for a quick second. "Okay, why don't you walk out of the airport to the main road leading to the freeway and find a taxi there?"

She got testy. "No, I cannot walk out of the airport area to the freeway. If I had known that you wouldn't come get me, I wouldn't have five-inch heels on. And my luggage is heavy."

"Really?" Favor probed. "Would it help if you walked slowly to the freeway? Or could you refuse to pay the airport taxicabs their rate? Tell them it's too much!"

Click. She hung up on him.

Example #4:

It was 93 degrees Fahrenheit in the shade. Inside the house, it was like 100. The power was out. A sweltering Favor lay on his bed in his bedroom. He was down to his boxer shorts and nothing else.

After about an hour of this, he went downstairs and out into the backyard where the generator was kept. He checked the diesel level. It was full. He looked at his watch. It was 8:34 p.m.

He went back indoors and upstairs to his swelteringly hot bedroom to lie down again.

Example #5:

Favor's old girlfriend came by to visit him on a Tuesday morning. Of course, she knew he was home because he had mentioned to her that he was going to be on vacation that week.

He was glad she had come by; since she got married, his fondness for her had increased. As far as he could ascertain, she was still in love with him.

They sat companionably in his front room. A soccer game was on, and he tried to split his attention between her and the television. After about fifteen minutes, Favor said to her: "I would have offered you something to drink, but I know you women are always minding your figures… so no need to, right?"

Igbo tradition in some regions dictates that, *ndi ichie* and the *Eze* cannot eat yams peeled and cooked by a woman.

Therefore, a male must cook the yams upon a wood fire set within a circle drawn with *nzu*, into which women are forbidden to step. When the yams are done, the cook dishes and serves the meal to the titled men.

Truth of the matter is that, in the ancient past when the women cooked the yams, little or none of the savory meal managed to escape the kitchen.

They were in the marriage counselor's office: a very angry wife and her somewhat confused husband. It was evening, and the sun was rapidly sinking below the horizon of trees in the distance. The last radiant glow of the setting sun gave a golden hue to almost everything in the room, as if to say, "Here, you are special. Remember this moment well!"

Mofe remained silent and attentive, as he listened to his wife vent her feelings and thoughts. Abayomi was extremely angry because she had just discovered from her coworkers that Mofe had been having several extramarital affairs – after twenty-plus years of marriage. Her own Mofe, of whom she boasted all day long to anyone who cared to listen. The details – who, when, where – she did not yet have; that was why there were here. Furthermore, Mofe had the effrontery to insist to her that he had had all those affairs for *her* sake?

The counselor listened very patiently to Abayomi's outburst of anger, clucking with sympathy at the right moments, and letting her talk until she could speak no more.

Handing more tissue paper to Abayomi, the counselor finally turned to Mofe and asked for his side of the story. It was a simple thing, Mofe said: It was all for her. He knew how status driven his wife was, even right from their college days when they were campus sweethearts. Even way back then, Mofe shared, he had promised to do everything within his power to make her successful. When Abayomi was successful, she was happy. When Abayomi was happy, he was happy. Mofe explained that he had no other motive for living apart from his wife.

Mofe had made himself quite comfortable with his role as the house-husband. He was never involved in any family or neighborhood controversies. He shopped, cooked, laundered and handled the repairs around the house. He kept their home and children immaculately clean and ordered. He was the one the children went to for help with their homework and extracurricular activities; they never bothered "Mummy". Astonishingly, Mofe never sought the limelight for all the work he did around the home. Even when his male friends made good-natured jokes about his

18

masculinity, and who really wore the pants in their relationship, Mofe took it all in stride. He was dedicated to Abayomi, and to her only. That was that. So when Abayomi got a corporate job after graduation, it seemed only natural for Mofe to stay at home, care for the kids that came along, and continue to be his wife's support.

"So how could you? Mofe, twenty-five different people! How could you be sleeping with all these people and still claim that you live only for me?" Abayomi cried.

"Abayomi, I have loved no other woman in my life besides you. I did and still do everything for you," he insisted.

"How would you feel if it were I who had been sleeping around with all these people, huh? How would you have felt?"

Looking at her with quiet eyes, he responded, "If it brought you happiness, then I would have no complaints."

"Look at me, Mofe! Just look at me now! I am the laughingstock of my peers, subordinates and superiors at work! How can I ever live this down?"

"No one is laughing at you, Abayomi. Only those involved know. No one else is privy to what has happened."

Abayomi burst into tears. She cried so hard that when the room suddenly became dark from the setting sun, it was as if it had said, "I can't bear watching this scene!" and dove out of sight. Mofe knew better than to try putting his arms around her in this state. He just watched as she bawled her eyes out.

The counselor spoke. "Mofe, I believe now would be a good time to tell Abayomi why you slept with all these people at her place of work. She needs to know. She needs to hear and process this information before she can move on."

Mofe sighed deeply and looked out the window. It was dark, but the darkness could not match the darkness inside his heart at that moment. Tears flooded his eyes as turned to Abayomi.

"Abayomi, I am truly and deeply sorry that you have been hurt by this revelation. It was never my intention to make you feel this way. If I could take it all back, I would. But do believe me when I still say that I did it all for you. I wanted you to do well. I wanted you to excel. I wanted you to be powerful. I wanted doors to open for you, for golden opportunities to come your way. But how could I, Mofe-who-stays-at-home-Mofe, Mofe-who-knows-nobody-Mofe, Mofe-with-nothing-of-his-own-Mofe, do anything for you?"

"Many, many years ago, I was at home alone watching Oprah, I had an idea from the show. She was interviewing women who had cheated on their husbands in order to help build their husbands' businesses. I said to myself, "Why not do the same for my wife? You've told me so many times that I'm good in bed, and with the free time I had on my hands after the kids went to school, I could read books and watch tapes on how to better my skills. Remember how some years ago you started complimenting me on my bedroom skills? That was a side benefit of all my personal education in this arena."

He paused to wipe his teary eyes with the back of his hand. Abayomi had stopped crying. She and the counselor listened with rapt attention.

"Go on," urged the counselor.

Mofe took a deep breath. "So when I built up my confidence, I approached your first supervisor at work."

Abayomi gasped. "You what?"

"Yes, I approached your very first supervisor," Abayomi repeated. "Do you remember Violet, head of the sales department? The one who made your life a living hell? I called her. I talked with her, and over a period of several weeks, I became intimate with her. I was able to find out from her what she didn't like about you, and gradually convinced her that you were a very likeable person and valuable employee. Eventually, she shared with me what you needed to do to get ahead within your company. Remember how I often asked you how your day went, then offered you bull's-eye advice on your situation? It was because I had already heard firsthand from the horse's mouth."

"I know that it sounds strange and unbelievable, but it worked. Violet recommended you for advanced training and eventually, a well-deserved promotion. Finally, I felt like I was contributing to your success in a concrete and tangible way. And as you climbed the corporate ladder, I systematically sought out and befriended your bosses. I gave them what they liked, and they gave me what I wanted – your progress to the top."

The silence in the room was heavy with emotion. Mofe could hear his own heart beating as his eyes searched his wife's face for any signs of understanding.

The counselor had never heard anything like this in practice before. "Surely not all of Abayomi's bosses were female?" the counselor enquired. "How did you influence her male supervisors?"

Mofe turned and looked the counselor square in the eye. "Men need love too, you know."

Abayomi fainted.

In the Name of Allah, the Merciful, the Compassionate.

I am submitted.

Is this still my home, my land?

Are these still my parents and my siblings?

Where are my children, the fruits of my labor?

I sit here barren, an orphan in the midst of communal feasting.

Is this still my love, my destiny?

Where is the rest that was promised me by the prophets?

The horizon is hazy through the dust in my tears.

Naked have I come. Naked must I go

Back to my Beloved.

The Nomads

The muezzin calls to the faithful to prayer. The journey calls the nomads to embark. The dusty desert trail leads to Oasis #2, #3, #4… or possibly a wicked silvery mirage – they know not for sure. But this is the only life they've known: A start, a stop, a look-see, a moving-on. Their camels plod along that trail: diffident and surefooted among the stony rubble of cities lost; fortresses destroyed; vegetation razed; wells run dry.

Night falls, and the trail goes cold at Oasis #2. The nomads are grateful for this. At the Pool of Apperception, the nomads pause for self-reflection, as is their custom. They drink from the feeding stream, but on one knee and with both eyes open. After supper, they gather by firelight to pore over treasure maps and swap tales of ancient glorious empires. From one another, the nomads seek an arcane knowledge, a deep-seated wisdom; one which will release them to grow roots in their ultimate homelands. One by one, they finally fall asleep ensconced in their rugs.

Dawn steals across the oriental skies, and the nomads resume their journey. Their anticipation rises with the sun. One of them looks wonderingly one way; the other, bravely the other way; yet another looks back with longing. Each viewed vista appears promising. But the price of uncertainty bands them together, for survival.

At the solar zenith, their expectations famish with the disappearance of the dew. They raise a makeshift shelter to rest, and to wait awhile. Lifting their faces, the nomads attempt to divine the skies of their fortunes. They talk among themselves; what color of sky portends the best option for their journey?

A courageous one among their band decides to strike out alone to an oasis, but she is not quite sure of its route. But try she must. The other nomads cry, "Wait!" She waits not. Covering her face against the desert winds and sun, she dashes forward. But a hundred feet away, she collapses from the aridity of loneliness. With her last conscious breath, she cries out, "Save me!" One of her fellows rushes forth to rescue her. He drags her back to shelter; wraps her in cool linen cloths; wets her forehead with precious water; commands her, "Live!" She lives. The nomads admonish her. She cries. It was an inner call to root that she sought to answer. The nomads decide to stay awhile in this one place, until the sand storms cease their howling.

Night falls again over the camp of the wandering, restless ones. The melody of a flute rises, sinks, rises again, and then fades away into the still, cold desert air. They are silent, each communing with a million elusive thoughts. But she is alert, remembering the call to root here, somewhere, now. What did that mean – an abandonment of her nomadic way of life? Risking pain, failure and disappointment at the impermanence of existence?

In the Name of Allah, the Merciful, the Compassionate.

I am submitted.

One by one, two by two,

To them all does my Beloved still sells.

I wait my turn as the night swiftly wipes the sky.

One by one, two by two,

Each basket is filled with diverse parcels

Still confident, I know not what mine will contain.

One by one, two by two,

There are murmurs, some outright grumbles

But like a few others, I will be imperfectly grateful.

One by one, two by two,

Masses milling about the multitude of mud shops

While my Beloved sells to those who find the master shop.

Woman Number 1: Women should stop depending on men to make it in life. Women should make their own money. Rich women can practically choose their own man – young, old poor, rich, educated or traveled.

Woman Number 2: A woman's status still depends on her having her own family. Marriage and children give dignity to a woman in our society, regardless of tribe, financial or educational level. It is good for a woman to answer to a man's name, even as a second, third, fourth or fifth wife... or even as a concubine.

Woman Number 3: Whether you are married or not, the best thing is to catch a senator, governor or other rich politician who will give you the money or set you up with contracts to maintain yourself. If you cannot get a 'happening' guy here, then target the ones overseas.

Woman Number 4: During our last deliverance, our pastor said that God gives true husbands to those women who are submissive and obedient. We must wait on the Lord for His own good time. In the meantime, Jesus is my husband!

Woman Number 5: Everybody knows that you can use a concoction to catch a man. After all, how do all those ugly *ashewo* women marry all those good men while the church ladies remain single? 'Remote control' still works!

Woman Number 6: Have you forgotten that without a husband, your children will find it difficult to marry another Nigerian? Where will your son take possession and build his own homestead? Who will receive your daughter's bride price?

Woman Number 7: What if I choose not to marry and not to have children?

Woman Number 2: Who will take care of you in your old age?

Woman Number 1: Who will takeover your property after you die?

Woman Number 4: Can you join the Christian Mother's Guild or the Mothers of Faith group?

Woman Number 6: Why be so selfish? Didn't someone bring you into this world?

Woman Number 5: Do you want to be called a frustrated woman?

Woman Number 3: How can you survive without a man?

Ridiculosity

A day can start with ridiculousity. It doesn't have to end the same way. Just find a way to kill it before it grows into an uncontrollable, fire-breathing dragon that will consume you.

Ridiculousity can be contagious if you're not careful. A few mornings ago, I was sipping my morning tea and minding my own business when Karla came out to ask me about the Cristal champagne box from the day before. Now, these boxes are not spectacular – they're made of cardboard, have a plush white interior, and come with a little booklet about the wine.

So, back to the day before. Karla, her husband Victor and I had picked up a male friend of theirs, Babuali on the drive to some village traditional wedding. The manner of these events was that city dwellers would throw these lavish parties in the countryside ostensibly to fulfill their local culture – and the village folks.

Soon enough, we get there with more of their friends. The setting sun is still hot. We make a grand entrance holding our own tin Moet goblets in hand. We are drenched in sweat. Our hosts are supposed to be impressed. Victor and his friends commandeer chairs for us all. Drinks are everywhere. Victor and his friends loudly demand for champagne and party favors. My clothes are soaked and I make no pretense of having any more makeup on. The champagne arrives. We start popping. Music is blaring. Two hundred or so people are milling around.

Then the Cristal arrives in a golden box with a silver latch.

Me, I'm practical-minded. I can already see in my mind's eye what use to which I can put this box – jewelry, gift, decoration, a show-and-tell. I ask Babuali what he thinks. Without hesitation, he gives it to me and I stow it away in my party favor bag. I'm pleased at my ingenuity.

One half hour later, Victor says it's time to go. I pick up my bag. Espying the golden box, Victor wants to know: Am I leaving the party with a bottle of Cristal? No, I explain to him what I have in mind. He exclaims, "No don't do that! Leave it behind! People will see you and think that you are leaving with the host's Cristal!"

Oh. I retrieve the empty box and drop it on the sandy ground. Thanks for letting me know.

Back to my morning tea… and Karla.

"So what were you intending to do with the box?"

"Oh, I though it would make a great travel case for my jewelry or fragile items. It has a great padded interior."

Karla rolled her eyes and fluttered her long fake lashes. "Are you out of your mind? How classless of you! I swear to my heavenly father if I had seen you with that box I would have gotten up from my seat and moved away! Oh my god, what a disgrace. I wouldn't even want to be seen in the same vehicle with you. That was so classless of you. A Cristal champagne box? In public? And then people would see you and say, "Look at this one leaving with drinks!" How could you take a bottle of Cristal champagne? I swear to God, if someone is my friend I would never let them disgrace me like that. That's why I don't make friends easily…"

"Really? Like, really, Karla? All this for an empty box? And besides, who knows me anyhow? I don't live here, and I wasn't aware of your cultural thing about this. Besides, I did ask Babuali – your friend – if it was okay and he gave it to me."

"You asked who? Babuali who? That classless man? Oh my God! What a disgrace! I can't believe you're saying this. And what cultural thing? Aren't you one of us?"

Ridiculousity in full steam. The full worth of a bottle of champagne being imposed on its worthless box. I got up to leave.

"Oh, by the way, would you happen to have seven thousand naira on you by any chance? I need to give my driver to make some purchases for me. And could you please accompany me to a nearby town to look at some project I'm working on? You know you're so intelligent and I'd like you to see it to give me your input."

For a moment, I looked at her bright, fake smile. I was angry, but I kept a deadpan expression as I reached into my purse, took out the money and handed it to her. Then I walked away.

People will come at you with their bullshit drama to cover up their complexes, feelings of insecurity, of being 'found out' for what they truly are. Remember, it's all their drama, not yours. Breathe deep, breathe long. Take a long stretch. Roll your head around in circles. Look at something blue or green. Walk away. Maintain mental equilibrium, no matter what.

It was time to go to bed. I had missed the chance at a sleeping spot in my fave uncle's house, so I had to move on to a recently late granduncle's house nearby. This would not have been so bad, had it not been for the fact that he – the late granduncle, of course – had been buried underneath his bedroom floor. I wanted nothing to do with dead people! Added to this was the earlier event of that afternoon: a small, black snake had been killed in the bedroom of his adult grandson, Chidoma. Chidoma had been hysterical and fled the scene; his cousins and nephews took care of it and brought him back home, to the amusement of the women and girls. But we all had a soft spot for Chidoma; he was quite handsome, tall and very kind-hearted. He was the sort to give you the last shirt off his back.

Well, it was time to go to sleep. There were several of us relatives who had sat out in the living room telling tales and recounting stories from Christmases past. A little bit about the living room of this house: there were wide metal grills on all the windows, as well as a movable metal grill for the main door. These were customary for protection against potential intruders. Furthermore, since this was in deep countryside, there was no electricity. We had a couple of kerosene lanterns and some candles for light. Food was regularly cooked over big, open fires fed by firewood from the bush.

Again, time to sleep. Some relatives left for their sleeping spots elsewhere; ten of us settled down on two king-sized mattresses laid in the middle of the living room floor. Chidoma locked the metal grill against the door. The lanterns and candles were extinguished as Chidoma found his way to the end of the mattress where I lay.

Within several minutes, diverse sounds of sleep filled the air: gurgles, snores, grunts and mumblings. I was still wide-awake in the darkness. I tossed and turned as I thought about our granduncle's grave barely a stone's throw from where I lay. I thought about the spirit-world I had heard so much about from my cousins; I wondered if our grand-uncle was just as stern over there with them as he had been with us over here during his lifetime.

I turned over onto my back. Peering through the darkness, I saw a white mist, a white 'something' beginning to coalesce up in the air above me. Could that be the spirit of our granduncle? I lightly touched Chidoma to make sure that he was still there beside me; I didn't want to find myself in spirit-land before my time! TI watched as the white thing started descending slowly toward my head. I panicked, grabbed Chidoma and yelped.

Within what seemed like a twinkle of an eye, Chidoma had leaped up from his spot yelling that there was a huge snake, a python, in the room with us. Others awoke in the pitch darkness and started screaming too. Only one younger cousin lay in deep sleep on the mattresses, oblivious to the mayhem. Those who were awake jumped up to get away from the mattresses. I held tight onto Chidoma's legs as he fled into some corner of the darkness, dragging me along. The screaming and crying intensified. Chidoma was still screaming over and over again for someone to bring a light, because there was a python in the room trying to strangle him alive. I was still screaming over and over again for help from the white thing trying to attack me. The younger cousin still slept as others ran about in the utter darkness screaming for light, God, mummy, daddy, weapons, water, whatever.

There was pounding at the front door. No one inside could open it because it had been locked and no one knew where the key was in the darkness. The screaming continued, unabated. The single pounding at the door became multiple poundings, with people outside shouting for us to open the door for them to see what was going on. Then a wide, powerful beam of light shone through one of the windows – from a flashlight held by Brother Adam. He swept it from side to side, and we could now see ourselves, in various states of dishevelment.

The screaming stopped. Brother Adam called Chidoma. Chidoma responded. Everyone, except our sleeping cousin, wanted to know who started the confusion. Brother Adam called me. I responded. He demanded to know who had died. Chidoma said it was I screaming about spirits; I said it was him screaming about pythons. The python was my two arms around Chidoma's thighs. The white thing was my overactive imagination. People laughed and left. We all went back to sleep, knowing that this was now going to be a Christmas joke staple for years to come.

I loved living in the village! Why bother with the city and all of its *"Pay for this! Pay for that!"* when village entertainment was both live and free? In particular, we had the **'Sunday-Sunday merecin'**. Just like the once-a-week, 'Sunday-Sunday medicine', the malarial prophylactic that everyone was unfailingly required to take to help ward off acute malarial attacks, each weekend – every blessed weekend, more often on a Sunday than not, without fail – there was always some drama happening somewhere in somebody's family that was enacted to the enjoyment of all, albeit to the chagrin of the participants.

Take one Sunday, for instance, as we hung around our uncle Ete's house, waiting for nothing in particular to happen. Our ears and eyes were open nevertheless. Eddie had been in an argument with his father Ete, about allowing him to drive the family car. In short, Eddie wanted Ete to give him – *the first born son* – the car keys so that he could drive out to wherever, just like other firstborn sons in other families. Ete refused, and for good reason too; the two-door, rusting, French-made *Citroen* was the only working car the family had. Eddie was not exactly known for his careful ways, so why tempt fate to undo the family in one fell swoop?

Tempers flared between son and father. Manly voices rose to the skies. Outrageous comparisons were made. Eddie decided that enough was enough – he was going to commit suicide so that "Ete could enjoy his property all by himself".

Suicide? Ete started laughing hysterically. Baby streams of tears ran down his wizened cheeks as his body convulsed with mirth. The rest of us watched in amazement as Eddie, even more furious, first ran toward his bedroom, then to the kitchen. He finally leaped atop a bench in front of the kitchen, brandishing a table knife in his right hand. His mother, Aunty, looked at him, screamed and started crying that somebody should do something to stop the madness. Some of the young female relatives joined her crying. Ete laughed louder, even more hysterically, as he shouted, "Everybody come o! Come see Sunday-Sunday merecin o!"

Other relatives started hastening to the scene. Eddie announced that he was going to commit suicide – yes, *suicide* – in full view of his father's compound so that the family would know the extent of Ete's inhumanity to the children of his own loins. He shouted about how he – yes, he, Eddie – had been a model son – a claim which was buffeted by guffaws of incredulous laughter from Ete and snickers from the rest of us onlookers – but apparently, that stellar reputation was insufficient for his own father.

Some relatives told Eddie to shut up, others pleaded that he shouldn't say such things – after all, he knew the tradition. Suicide was an abomination and if he did kill himself, his cursed body could not be buried; it would have to be thrown away into the local forest for the evil spirits to devour.

Eddie would not relent. He was the first born son, he insisted, and he was entitled to his inheritance. Ete asked him to define the word 'inheritance'. Eddie said it meant 'father's property'. Ete called him a fool – inheritance was what you got left to you after the death of someone, not while the person was alive; so if he, Eddie, wanted his 'inheritance' from him, Ete, then he, Eddie, should come kill him first. The relatives raised a hue and cry, "Chei! Abomination! Eddie, will you kill your own father because of a *car*?"

Even as Eddie tried to argue himself out of that verbal mess, his three younger brothers – the triplets – were in the background, picking over his few clothes. Not wanting to waste any precious time, they had quickly run into his bedroom to grab as many of his serviceable clothing as they could lay their little grubby hands on. Most importantly, there was this pair of jeans that Eddie had received as a gift from one of their older sisters in London. The jeans had been purchased '*overseas*'; this made it quite precious. The triplets bickered over the pants, two pulling a leg each and the other the waist. Each insisted that the other should let go. (Truth be told, Eddie had promised it to each of them (in private) for past favors.) Their fight over these '*overseas*' jeans got so loud that Eddie had to stop in the middle of one of his pre-suicide speeches and yell at them to put the jeans down or face his wrath. Immediately, they dropped the thing and slunk away to safety, leaving their other gains behind. After all, they didn't want Eddie to kill them before committing suicide!

The sun was slow in setting. Ete pointed to his watch and reminded Eddie that dinnertime was fast approaching, so could he please hurry up with his suicide so that the the rest of the family would have more food to share? Eddie started shouting again, calling to all and sundry to come hear what his father was saying to him. Ete turned to the triplets and reassured them that, with Eddie dead and out of the way, they would have more to eat and drink.

"Yay!" chimed the boys, "But who will get the 'overseas' jeans?"

The oldest triplet asked, "Ete, if Eddie dies, I will be your first-born son, right?"

Dede laughed and agreed.

The other two grumbled. "What kind of first-born? We are all age-mates o! We will not obey you! We will share everything equally! Ete, tell him o!"

It was time to die, publicly, Eddie announced. He applied the table knife-edge to his left wrist and started sawing away with vigor. On seeing this, his mother became hysterical and fell to the ground, shrieking. Relatives, surrounding her, struggled to raise her up off the ground.

More commotion ensued though no one actually came forward to stop Eddie. Instead, they ran up to Ete to do something. Ete kept shouting at him, "Eddie, what are you waiting for? Die now! Die now! I want to see you die now so that I know how many actual children I have left! *Die, Eddie! Die! I say, die now! Die so that I can rest!*"

Eddie continued sawing at his wrist. No blood spurted. None trickled. There wasn't even a mark! Ete kept shouting at him to hurry up. In the midst of this drama, I crept up to Eddie on his bench and observed that he was applying the blunt edge of the table knife at an angle to his skin. I knew what the problem was... and I knew what the solution was as well!

So just trying to be helpful, I pointed out to Eddie that he wasn't using the knife properly. His skin would not cut easily that way; why not use the serrated edge at right angles to his wrist, directly over one of the veins? That way, I assured him, he was sure to get immediate results.

36

Eddie turned to look at me with angry, incredulous eyes. He started screaming at me like I was the enemy.

"Did I ask you? Eh, who asked you to show me how to cut myself? Ehn, who asked you? Is it your hand? Busybody! Pokenoser! See me see trouble? Who asked you? Get away from here! Don't let me slap you o! Idiot!"

And with that, he got off the bench, went into his bedroom and slammed the door to resounding laughter from everyone and cries of "Sunday-Sunday merecin!"

Uncle Kilompa used to stand by the rocks at Bar Beach, looking pensively at the wild waves that beat the rocks as if they were fighting over money. He wore his suit with open-toed sandals. He always wore the same suit: a dark, greenish brown affair of indeterminate material. That didn't matter, anyhow. It was rumored that Uncle had 35 suits, all the same size and color. No one knew why, but it was said that that was how they did things in England. A distinguished man was made the more distinguished by his distinguished suits. And Uncle had most certainly been to England many times, it was said by those who knew about these things.

We children always thought the world of Uncle. Every Sunday after church, our parents would take us to his third floor flat. Auntie Ada, Uncle's wife, made sure that there was rice and stew aplenty, waiting for our hungry little bellies. We would hug both of them upon entrance into the small flat; thereafter, we were shooed to the back balcony to go play while the adults sat down and discussed important things that were not meant for our ears.

When our huge tray of food finally arrived at the back, we sat and devoured everything without ceremony – rice, chicken and bones. The bones were the best. First you chewed off the soft, knobby ends, then you sucked the marrow out of the bone. If the marrow resisted, you cracked open the shank of the bone to reveal the marrow and suck away. Only the hardest bits of bone got discarded; every thing else was chewed and swallowed.

After eating, the adults would call us to the parlor to dance for them. It was always a dancing competition. The winner got one stick of Miki Miki, that stick of delectable caramel candy. Uncle Kilompa would pull out the one black vinyl record that was sure to elicit the most effort from us: James Brown's "Get On Up". Back then, we knew it as the 'Kilompa' record.

With the record duly selected, we children would take up our positions on the impromptu dance floor; you always needed the best space to clearly demonstrate your best moves. You also pre-warned your compadres not to interfere with your dancing space, or else!

Uncle Kilompa carefully placed the vinyl record on the turntable. Then, with great dignity, he lifted and placed the stylus on the outer rim of the record,. The record started spinning. There was a pause as the crackling noise from the record filled the room... then it was time for us to get down to James Brown's exhortations:

"Fellas, I'm ready to get up and do my thing (yeah go ahead!)

I wanta get into it, man, you know (go ahead!)

Like a, like a sex machine, man, (yeah go ahead!)

Movin' and doin' it, you know

Can I count it off? (Go ahead)"

"One, two, three, four!

Get up, (get on up)

Get up, (get on up)

Stay on the scene, (get on up),

Like a sex machine, (get on up)"

At the same time, all of us the children sang along with Mr. Brown:

"One, two, three, four!

Kilompa, kilore!

Kilompa, kilore!

Kilon machine eh, kilore!

I wanna send machine eh, kilore!"

The adults laughed with hysteria as we jumped, twisted, whirled and bent to the beat. A little bit of pushing and shoving, someone crying in the corner. Very soon, we were sweating in our Sunday best. We were determined to win that Miki Miki. The adults pointed and encouraged us by name to dance harder. We danced harder. One of my older cousins – in an effort to distinguish himself from the rest of us – leaped into the air and landed on his butt. The adults roared out in laughter. The rest of us snickered and kept on inventing new moves.

The record eventually came to an end. With much fanfare and congratulatory speeches by the adults, Uncle Kilompa announced that it was too hard to determine the true winner of the dancing competition. He always said that, every time we came to his house to dance. We protested loudly, as usual. Some of us rolled our eyes. Some of us hissed, albeit softly for fear of instant retribution from the adults.

In the end, that one slender stick of delectable caramel candy was tweezed into bits by Auntie Ada and shared among all of us children present. Each one of us took our minuscule bit of Miki Miki with much happiness and popped it into our mouths right away.

We all had done well. We all deserved the prize.

Kilompa, kilore!

Part One:

I am satisfied. I have done what I am required to do.

Here is the night before the ancient resurrection.

The relinquishing of the dusty, banal cloak

In exchange for the mystical wings of mystery.

So, in worldly silence, I wait with patience

Through the dark leading into the dawn of the sacred day.

Part Two:

The fear of death permeates the air of the faithless few.

The surety of resurrection buoys my passage through

The recurrent dramatic illusions of this world, lustily echoed

In the triad of blessings and curses of the saints of old.

I smile. Surely fulfillment of the law is never futile

And should be plain to see by those with percipience.

Part Three:

I approach the dark grave, the altar of terrestriality

Knowing full well that existence must be fulfilled

As must, death to one realm preceding life in another,

Soul by soul, age upon age. The tale of remembrance told,

The drama of instructions enacted – it is done!

I rise, born anew – shriven, hallowed, crowned and exalted.

www.ingramcontent.com/pod-product-compliance
Lightning Source LLC
Chambersburg PA
CBHW071222130626
46555CB00004B/1800